POV: I'm a Nurse

Michelle Bautista

BookLeaf Publishing

Presentation by *BookLeaf Publishing*

Web: www.bookleafpub.com

E-mail: info@bookleafpub.com

ISBN: 978-93-95755-67-2

First edition 2022

To my future self...

Please don't ever be callous as an RN.

ACKNOWLEDGEMENT

First of all, I would like to acknowledge the sacrifices of my parents, Benedicto and Sofia, who did everything they could to get me through the best school for my Bachelors of Science in Nursing, and for supporting me in my move to Australia. Without them, these precious experiences wouldn't have been possible.

I would also like to acknowledge and thank both my sister, Mary Jane, and my husband, Jeene-von, your support has always strengthen me.

Also, I would like to acknowledge the different people to whom I've worked with, to whom I've been given the opportunity to take care of, in the past decade, or so.

Finally, I acknowledge our God above, for giving me all the provisions and opportunities in life.

PREFACE

This book of poems has been inspired after more than a decade of being in the field of nursing. During those times, I have experienced the celebration of life, the suffering and/or overcoming of illnesses, and the succumbing to death.

However, I acknowledge that these do not represent the feelings and thoughts of everyone in the healthcare profession.

-Michelle S. Bautista, RN
Beechworth VIC

Home

I walked to the east,
But my anxiety increased.

I walked to the south,
But there are places i'm not allowed.

I walked to the west,
But I can't seem to rest.

I walked to the north,
But for what it's worth?

I wanna go home,
But the nurse said i'm home.

I went back to the north,
But my tears started to burst.

Because when I search west,
My heart can't ever rest.

Whatever's in the south,
I can't remember what it's about.

I hope that when I go east,
I'll see the faces I know best.

I Was Her Superman

My legs may have been skinny and lanky,
But it used to be powerful and sturdy.
It goes wherever it needs and wherever she is,
It supported the weight of her joy and tears.
When we danced, I may have two left feet,
But her smile made me feel that I can dance to
the beat.
With these legs, I used to be able to do
everything for her.
But I lost all strength because of cancer.

My arms may have been hairy,
But it used to be brawny.
It allowed me to carry shopping bags and
groceries.
It allowed me to carry her and our babies.
When she's sad, she leans on my shoulder.
When she's happy, my arms envelopes her.
With these arms, I used to be able to do
everything for her.
But I lost all strength because of cancer.

My eyes may not be blue and pretty,
But these eyes see no one but her only.

It allowed me to capture every beautiful
moments of our life.
It allowed me to remember her face, her laugh,
her smile.
In sadness, we've shed some tears.
In joy, we still shed more tears.
When she lost her eyesight, I became her eyes
But with cancer, I lost my eyes.

I used to be her superman,
Her number one fan,
The one who always can.
I'm supposed to be her carer,
But now I can't 'cause of cancer.

Abyss

Outside I was laughing,
Though inside I am hurting.
The sun is shining,
But in my heart is raining.

I am trapped in a pool so deep,
Attached to a ball of steel.
The pool which is made of glass,
Unbreakable, though you hit with brass.

Try to swim up
From an endless cup.
Try to speak up,
Nothing comes up.

It's not easy to release
But who would like a piece?
This burden's so dark and heavy
No one could seem to carry.

What if I hold my breath?
I must escape through death.
This darkness might then end.
From the abyss I might ascend.

With The Fairies

There's a stranger in my room,
Came with tablets of doom.
Introduced her name as Kerry
And said "I'm your nurse today, Harry."

Bitter in my taste,
I think they are laced.
A few minutes has passed,
I'm now having a blast.

The grey sky turned blue,
I see the place anew.
No longer agitated.
My temper has abated.

My mood which was previously low,
Has changed as if everything glow.
I can't remember what I'm here for,
But it's okay, I won't roar anymore.

To Send Off With A Smile

Have you ever had someone
Who's not even your family
But has occupied a special place in your heart,
And has made your work-life worthwhile?

As a patient, they've been the most pleasant;
Despite the pain, they remained polite.
Though it's hard, they continue to smile.
And they always say,
"Thank you for caring for me."

As a resident, they've been most lovely;
Despite the pain, you're treated as an angel.
Though it's hard, their eyes always light up
when they see you.
And they never fail to say,
"Thank you for caring for me."

But like everything that has a start must also
end.
And after that rapport, a professional
relationship must always end.
This is something you would always expect.
Remember, change is the only constant in life.

With hospital patients often going home when
they get better.
But unfortunately there are some who don't
make it.
Despite that, you will smile for those who are
living and leaving.
While stay strong for those that're left behind.

On the other hand, there are only two reasons for
residents to leave aged care.
One is when they're transferred somewhere else,
Another is when they pass away.
Again, you smile for the living while stay strong
for the families that're left behind.

Metamorphosis

One by one…she changed.

She's losing her hair.
It used to be luscious,
Wavy and black.
With each comb
They fall on the floor.

Her lips are now cracked.
It used to be plump and pink.
Tasted of sugar and honey.
With each breath,
Is a gasp for more air.

Her eyes looked swollen.
It used to be bright and gorgeous.
Like two inviting chocolates.
With each movement,
Tears come streaming down.

She's now bedridden.
She used to be able to dance.
Lively, joyous, energetic.
Her arms and legs have failed her,
Everything feels like a punishment.

She easily gets angry.
She used to be very pleasant.
Calm, understanding, happy.
She feels pain everywhere,
She thinks, "They don't understand me."

The Masquerade

My wife, my lovely wife
Has lost her lustre and hope
Though I'm the same
I need to stay sane

Put on a mask I must.
Smile before she bust,
Cause i'm her strength
Despite the length.

I must act strong
But then how long?
Oh God, I pray
That I could keep this play.

Whenever she cry,
Inside I die.
Tell her it's okay,
I'm lying everyday.

Sandcastle

When I was born,
My parents had high hopes for me.
To grow up healthy,
And also be happy.

When I was in school,
My teachers had high hopes for me.
To earn some skills and knowledge,
And also go to college.

When I was in college,
My professors had high hopes for me.
To learn my future trade,
And in the future get paid.

When I graduated,
I had high hopes for myself.
To get a good job,
And be like the higher mob.

All these I attained,
I steered and reigned.
I struggled but prevailed
I may have cried but never bailed.

When I created a family,
We had high hopes for us.
Went forth and multiplied,
I tell you, it wasn't an easy stride.

And my parent's hopes
Became our hopes
And the cycle goes
But only God knows.

When I became older,
I still have high hopes for myself.
To rest and happily look back
At everything down the track.

Was I happy?
Or mostly sappy?
Was it worth it,
Too much, or a little bit?

I built my castle in the sand
But the waves that's coming is grand
My castle will fall and crumble
And I will be no more.

White Lie

"Where is my husband?"
She asked.
"He's already dead,
Two years ago," I said.

If I told her he's home
Might she just continue to roam?
Thinking she's not alone
Cause later he might phone.

"I wanna go home to my wife."
He insisted.
"But this is now your home,"
To him I answered.

If I told him he's in the hospital
Will I prevent his further spiral
Into sadness that can be lethal
And go back to being comical?

"I wanna go to the toilet unassisted,"
She told me as she continuously failed.
"But you can't walk no more,"
I told her as we pick her off the floor.

But how do you tell someone
That they can no longer run?
"You're only paralysed for a moment?"
That won't be effective, I bet.

Photographic Memory

I wish I could forget
The day that we've met
Under that Venus statuette
In the orange sunset

When I look at the ocean,
I'm reminded of your eyes.
Not only it's as blue as yours,
But also so deep and full of emotion.

When I look at the sunny sky,
Oh it makes me sigh;
Like you, it's so beautiful and brilliant,
Certainly delightful in my sight.

When I feel the cool breeze,
Oh Lord, help me please!
Like your arms, it's soft and gentle
It's cold but pleasant, it's making me
sentimental!

When I look at our house,
I'm reminded that i'm now alone.
Your warmth that burns my heart
Is no more since we're apart.

Part B

The following collection of poems are tributes to my favourite patients, who has left their marks in my heart and mind. Some of them has already passed on, some of them are still living at the time these poems were made.

Furthermore, the remaining four poems are my tribute to my family.

Dear P. M.

Blind as you were,
yet your ears were sharp.
Bed might have imprisoned you,
yet your smile were free.

Your own blood may have turned their backs,
but you found family in us.
Stricken with pain so severe,
yet your song never fades.

I start to sing, and you'll start singing
Be it children's songs or old love songs,
Your sweet voice fills the room
Even though we're out of tune.

You came to my life,
And filled it with laughter.
And despite me being bitter,
In my mind you'll always linger..

Dear E. C.

To my number one fan
Together, we had fun.
I sing, you listen
We laugh and your eyes glisten.

Dementia has rendered you speechless,
And at times you were emotionless,
But when I sing, it's not useless
And casts a smile to your face that was lifeless.

It may have been brief
But your absence gives me grief.
Despite that i'm relieved,
Cause from suffering you're now released.

Dear V. R.

Our meeting may not be good when it started
Cause you were angry and broken-hearted
You were lost and confused
But after some time it has improved.

You're a great artist
Your skilful hand were excellent
And you've worked the hardest
Yet you always stayed modest.

Despite your pain, you're strong
Amidst your shortness of breath, you moved
along.
I have never heard you complain
Though I remind you not to tolerate it again and
again.

I may not be in your short-term memory,
But your behaviours are always exemplary
'Cause you've always been so kind to me.
So how could I leave you be?

Your body is now starting to fail
Though we might try to put it out
Only God knows when and what's about
So if you leave, I will definitely wail.

Dear K. B.

You are:

The definition of lost but happy,
The epitome of confused but pleasant,
The characterisation of the shining sun,
The essence of contentment,
The embodiment of kindness,
And the symbol of hope amidst illness.

I hope that you:
Keep your smile amidst the confusion
Remain good-natured despite feeling muddled
Stay bright like the sun
Maintain your serenity 'till the end
Persist being kind-hearted
And continue to be optimistic in spite of your
illness.

Dear R. D.

Your pain which never goes away
Never stopped you from being gay.
Your suffering which was so severe
Never stopped you from being a dear.

Your supposed three months were extended
That when it actually ended, we regretted.
Though our time may be short-lived
In my heart, you're always drilled.

The way you were always thankful
You've always been so delightful
How we've always been so grateful
And were also sorrowful.

Dear I. J.

Remember that time
When you opened up to me?
You were sad and lonely
Cause you're missing your one and only.

You told me about him,
Which has filled your love to the brim;
How worried was he
To ever leave you be.

But then he left this world,
With you alone and old.
And resulted to your fall
Which may have even be a close call.

I hugged you tight
As you try to fight
The tears that threatens
To fall in seconds.

Then she thanked me for my shoulder
And the way I consoled her.
Like a child she smiled
And together we laughed.

Dear I. J.,

For your kindness, I'll be thankful
For your secrets, I am grateful
For your blessing, I am fortunate.
I'm your friend, that is permanent.

Dear Mama

Rearing two children.
Must have been a burden;
I was neither a good daughter
I have sometimes sparked your anger.

We may have lacked money,
But you never let us go hungry.
And even when your budget's tight,
You gave us everything with all your might.

I'm thankful for carrying me for nine months,
I'm grateful for your sacrifices;
You could have other priorities,
Yet for us, you threw those opportunities.

Dear Papa

All your life you have toiled,
Overseas you stayed employed;
More than two decades of your life wasted
Persevered until we graduated.

In the desert as a cook,
Despite the heat you never shook.
To support your family you overtook,
Homesickness' not in the book.

In the snow as factory worker
Worked hard for various employer
Though there were times when problem arise,
But your hope is something that never dies.

I'm thankful for your support
Even though we were apart.
You could've other priorities,
Yet for us, you threw those opportunities.

Dear Jorge

In our younger years,
We've fought like tigers.
Now in our older year,
We're best friends forever.

I could never forget
And I am always in debt,
From your undying support
That has never fall short.

I pray you'd be happy
And try to be less snappy
Cause remember we are partners
Even when life gets harder.

To My Furless Cat

We may have started on the wrong foot,
Didn't believe we're meant to be,
I tried pushing you away,
But thankfully they're all in vain.

'Cause now you're the milk to my tea,
You're the sauce to my spaghetti,
You're the chips to my fish
And you're the page to my book.

I pray for your steadfast love,
Someone who will stay strong
And would still try to get along
In the midst of a storm that's me.